BULLETPROOF ACCOUNTING AND COMPLIANCE

21 PROVEN STRATEGIES

BULLETPROOF ACCOUNTING AND COMPLIANCE

21 PROVEN STRATEGIES

Chandan Goyal

Worldwide Published by
Pendown Press

PENDOWN PRESS LLP
An ISO 9001 & ISO 14001 Certified Co.,
Regd. Office: 3767A, Kanhaiya Nagar,
Tri Nagar, Delhi-110035
Ph.: 8130886000, 9650072927
E-mail: info@pendownpress.com
Branch Office: 1A/2A, 20, Hari Sadan, Ansari Road,
Daryaganj, New Delhi-110002
Ph.: 011-45794768
Website: PendownPress.com

Edition: 2025

ISBN: 978-93-6338-593-1

Layout and Cover Designed by Pendown Graphics Team
Printed and Bound in India by Thomson Press India Ltd.

Finance professionals navigating the complexities of their roles, this book is for you. Your hard work and commitment to excellence make a difference every day. May you find guidance and inspiration within these pages.

Contents

Acknowledgements

I am deeply grateful for the chance to share my experiences and insights with you. This book is the culmination of years of learning, growth, and dedication. I hope the words within these pages inspire, inform, and resonate with you.

I extend my heartfelt thanks to my parents. Your strength and wisdom have been instrumental in shaping my journey and contributing to my achievements.

To my wife, Dolly, you are not just my partner but the cornerstone of my strength. This accomplishment would not have been possible without your love and patience.

To my wonderful daughter, Aarvi, your laughter and joy fill my days with purpose and motivation. You inspire me to reach for the stars.

I am also thankful to my team members clients, mentors, colleagues, and the vibrant community of thinkers and doers. Your insights and support have played a crucial role in my growth and development. I owe much of my success to your invaluable guidance and encouragement.

A special thank you to my friend, Dinesh Verma, CEO of Pendown Press, and his team for their unwavering support and suggestions throughout the creative process.

To everyone mentioned and those who are not named, your contributions have been vital to my journey. Together, we have built something extraordinary, and I look forward to continuing this journey of growth and success with each of you.

Thank you for being a part of this shared experience.

Preface

In today's fast-paced business world, finance and accounting teams are expected to do far more than just crunch numbers. They play a critical role in shaping company strategy, ensuring compliance, and driving sustainable growth. This book aims to empower CFOs, finance controllers, and accounting professionals by providing clear and practical guidance on transforming processes, embracing innovation, and fostering continuous improvement.

The chapters in this book offer a comprehensive exploration of essential strategies, frameworks, and tools to elevate finance functions to new heights of efficiency and accuracy. From revolutionizing SOPs with video to harnessing automation through practical adaptations, each chapter provides actionable insights to improve day-to-day operations and achieve long-term success.

You'll also uncover the benefits of changing team roles to increase control and reduce risk, the value of setting precise quarterly goals, and the advantages of exposing finance professionals to the ground realities of business. The book further emphasizes the ATM framework—Accuracy, Timeliness, and Measurement—as a foundation for effective financial management.

Throughout these chapters, you'll find practical advice on building a high-performing team through training, development, and proactive team-building practices. You'll also explore how the critical tracking of AP parameters, the introduction of KPIs, and improved use of checklists can reduce errors, increase transparency, and enhance decision-making.

Whether you are a CFO, finance controller, or part of a finance team, the ideas shared in this book are plug-and-play strategies that are easy to adopt, regardless of your industry. By implementing these practices, you will not only improve your team's performance but also strengthen compliance, governance, and operational excellence.

As we explore the future of finance, remember that it's not just about mastering numbers; it's about mastering the tools, processes, and people behind those numbers. These practices will help you build a "bulletproof" finance function—one that withstands the challenges of today and thrives in the opportunities of tomorrow.

Thank you for picking up this book. Let's embark on this exciting journey toward financial excellence together!

Chandan Goyal

● ● ● ●

Introduction

Welcome to a resource that is poised to transform the way you approach accounting and compliance in your organization. Before we delve into the robust strategies and insights this book offers, allow me to introduce myself and share why I am passionate about empowering CFOs and finance professionals to achieve excellence in their roles.

My name is Chandan Goyal, and I bring over two decades of extensive experience in the accounting and compliance sector, having worked closely with more than 200 companies across various industries. This journey has not only honed my expertise in navigating complex financial landscapes but has also deepened my commitment to fostering robust accounting practices that drive business success.

Why You Can Trust My Advice

- ***Proven Track Record with Bestsellers:*** I am the author of two bestselling books, "How to Manufacture Time?" and "17 Instant Proven Cost Reduction Ideas." These publications have already helped thousands of professionals in enhancing their operational efficiencies and strategic capabilities, demonstrating my ability to convey complex concepts in an accessible manner.
- ***Extensive Practical Experience:*** Over the past 20 years, I have led a team of more than 100 professionals, providing tailored financial solutions that have consistently delivered results. This hands-on experience has equipped me with unique insights into the practical challenges and opportunities within the field of accounting and compliances.
- ***A Trusted Coach and Mentor:*** I have had the privilege of coaching over 1,350 CFOs and CEOs, focusing on cost

reduction and financial strategy. This role has allowed me to understand the diverse needs of businesses across various scales and sectors, making me adept at identifying universal challenges and crafting effective, scalable solutions.

- ***A Dedication to Giving Back:*** My motivation for writing this book is fueled by a desire to give back to the CFO community—a group that has been instrumental in my professional journey. By sharing the knowledge and strategies that I have accumulated, I aim to help other finance professionals strengthen their departments and achieve their business goals.

● ● ● ●

Why the Title "Bulletproof"?

At first glance, the title ***"Bulletproof"*** might bring to mind action-packed Bollywood movies where the hero, clad in a bulletproof jacket, faces danger head-on and narrowly escaping threats with the help of his trusted gear. This imagery isn't just for dramatic effect but serves as a powerful metaphor for the protective strategies we'll explore in this book.

In the world of accounting and compliance, finance professionals are not dodging actual bullets but are constantly under the threat of various metaphorical ones: delays, errors, fraud, over-dependence on certain team members, and the daunting consequences of non-compliance, such as penalties and interest charges. These challenges can disrupt even the most well-run finance departments. Just as a bulletproof vest is designed to protect vital organs, the practices and principles shared in this book are intended to shield your organization's financial health against the unexpected and often rapid-fire challenges that come your way.

The concept of being 'bulletproof' in finance doesn't imply a state of perfection where nothing can go wrong—rather, it's about building resilience and fortifying your systems so your department can withstand challenges without falling apart. It's about proactive protection—anticipating risks, reducing vulnerabilities, and enhancing the ability to perform under pressure with confidence.

The Bulletproof Philosophy

This book adopts a 'bulletproof philosophy' to business accounting and compliance, focusing on three key areas:

- ***Anticipation:*** Just as a bulletproof jacket is worn in anticipation of a threat, financial foresight involves anticipating problems before they manifest. This means staying updated with the latest in compliance regulations, forecasting financial trends, and preparing for end-of-year audits well in advance.

- ***Protection:*** Protection strategies involve setting up checks and balances that safeguard against errors and fraud. This includes implementing strong internal controls, conducting regular reconciliations, and employing state-of-the-art security measures to protect sensitive financial data.
- ***Resilience:*** Finally, resilience is about recovery and continuity. How quickly and efficiently can your finance team bounce back from setbacks? Enhancing resilience involves training, empowering your team through continuous learning, and creating a culture where mistakes are seen as opportunities for growth and improvement.

● ● ● ●

Why This Book Matters

The role of a CFO is filled with challenges—from navigating complex regulatory landscapes to managing intricate financial operations that impact the entire organizations. Throughout my career, I've observed patterns and practices that consistently yield positive results, enhancing both accuracy and reliability in financial departments. This book compiles those best practices, offering them as a resource for current and future finance leaders looking to protect their departments against the risks of today's dynamic business world.

How to Use This Book

Each chapter in this book is self-contained, addressing specific aspects of accounting and compliance. You don't need to read it from cover to cover—feel free to jump directly to whatever chapter interests you the most or addresses a challenge you're currently facing. Whether it's refining audit processes, leveraging technology for better data management, or enhancing team communication and planning, there's something here for every aspect of modern financial management.

The Promise of Practicality

The strategies outlined in this book are industry-agnostic, designed to provide value whether you're in manufacturing, retail, or any sector requiring robust financial oversight. They are presented as 'plug-and-play' solutions—ready to be implemented in your operations to save you hundreds of hours you might otherwise spend on trial and error. This practical approach is intended to offer immediate benefits, enhancing your efficiency and compliance with minimal adjustment time.

My Hope for You

My aim is simple: if you find even two or three ideas in this book that you can apply effectively, I will consider my mission accomplished. This book is designed not just to share knowledge but to inspire action and innovation. By implementing these proven strategies, you can not only safeguard your organization's financial operations but also elevate the strategic role of the finance department, ensuring it's not just a function of oversight but a cornerstone of business success.

Let's Begin

With each page, I invite you to explore practical, actionable strategies that are designed to protect and enhance your accounting and compliance functions. Here's to fewer financial surprises and more strategic triumphs as you apply these lessons to create a robust, efficient, and trustworthy financial operation.

Let's turn the page and start this journey together.

● ● ● ●

Words of Recognition

Bulletproof Accounting and Compliance is a must-read for CFOs, finance controllers, and accounting professionals seeking to elevate their performance and enhance delivery effectiveness. Chandan has distilled years of hands-on experience into practical strategies that are both actionable and inspiring. From leveraging automation and refining SOPs to fostering team resilience through role rotation and training, this book provides a comprehensive roadmap for transforming finance functions into strategic powerhouses.

If you're ready to streamline compliance, reduce risks, and turn your finance department into a driver of growth, this book will be your trusted companion on that journey.

Saurav Bhala,
Global Group CFO,
Sequent Scientific Ltd.

"Bulletproof Accounting and Compliance by Chandan Goyal is a treat to read for CFOs and their immediate leadership teams. He has beautifully articulated relevant, practical, and implementable ideas that every finance professional can relate to. While all the ideas in his book are simple, lucid, and highly relatable, I found the concept of the 'ATM Framework'—Accuracy, Timeliness, and Measurement—covered in Chapter 7, quite powerful.

This is a must-read and implement book for all finance professionals. Implementing the ideas proposed in the book will surely elevate the strategic contribution of the finance team in a meaningful way."

Neeraj Basur,
Group CFO

"Chandan has masterfully distilled the essentials of accounting and compliance best practices into a clear, insightful guide. This book is an invaluable resource for navigating today's complex regulatory landscape and is a must-read for professionals committed to excellence."

Kuljeet Singh,
Director Finance,
Gi Group India

"The handbook lives up to its title—21-gun salute to Chandan for capturing these strategies in such a clear and meticulous way. I am going to implement each one right away and reap the benefits for doing my role with ease and conviction. These are evergreen strategies, and I am sure Chandan will add more based on his understanding of market practices.

Thank you for providing CFOs with the arsenal to be the BEST in their roles—as strategists, compliant, and overall caretakers of the organization's financial health."

Ashish Lakhotia,
CFO,
Jagsonpal Pharmaceuticals Ltd.

"This book is a game-changer for finance professionals. The actionable strategies are simple to follow and make a real difference in daily operations. It is a must-read for CFOs looking to build a robust finance function."

G Surya Prakash,
Managing Director,
Propelor Pte Ltd.

Bulletproof Accounting and Compliance offers practical insights with easy-to-implement strategies that benefit both new and experienced professionals. We saw great results by converting SOPs to video and saving time through Assessment Readiness for audits. This book not only enhances efficiency but also inspires teams to think creatively and develop tailored solutions for their business needs.

Sanjay Goel,
Former CFO,
Barco India

Chapter 1

Revolutionizing SOPs with Video

In the fast-paced world of accounts and compliance, capturing and sharing knowledge effectively is crucial. Traditionally, Standard Operating Procedures (SOPs) have played a key role in maintaining consistency and ensuring that everyone knows what to do and how to do it. However, traditional SOPs can be cumbersome—filled with pages of text and screenshots, quickly becoming outdated, and often challenging to navigate.

Given that much of our accounting and compliance work is screen-based using different types of software, doesn't it make sense to have SOPs that reflect this reality?

Enter the era of Video SOPs.

The Game Changer: Video SOPs

Imagine watching a short video where someone demonstrates a process on-screen, in real-time. That's the beauty of Video SOPs. Created by the very people doing the job, they're authentic, practical, and easy to follow.

The process is simple. If you're an expert at reconciling accounts, for example, just use a virtual meeting platform like Zoom, Google Meet, or Microsoft Teams. Start a meeting with yourself, share your screen, hit record, and walk through the process as if you're teaching someone. Explain each step, why it's important, and offer any tips you've learned along the way.

Keep the videos concise—aim for 15-20 minutes. For complex processes, break them into smaller parts for easier digestion.

Addressing Staff Resistance

Initially, some staff may resist this new format. To encourage participation, consider rewarding employees who create high-quality, impactful Video SOPs. This approach not only encourages learning but also boosts engagement without incurring extra costs. Employees feel valued and are more likely to contribute actively.

Hosting with Ease

You might wonder, "Where do I put all these videos?" Teachable is a fantastic solution. This cloud-based platform is user-friendly for both uploaders and viewers, allows unlimited user accounts, and is affordable. Using Teachable, you can organize Video SOPs into courses, creating a structured, easily accessible digital library. New team member on board? Simply direct them to the relevant course on Teachable, and they're good to go.

The Bottom Line

Switching to Video SOPs revolutionizes how knowledge is transferred within your team. It makes learning interactive, engaging, and much less of a chore. As we move further into a digital age, our methods of sharing know-how need to keep pace. Embracing Video SOPs ensures your team has the tools they need to succeed, in a format that resonates with our digital-first world. So, grab your headset, start a meeting, and let's create a repository of knowledge that's helpful and enjoyable to use.

Conclusion

In conclusion, switching to Video SOPs is a smart and efficient way to train your team. They make learning faster, easier, and more engaging, especially in a digital world where most tasks are screen-based. With simple tools and minimal effort, you can create a library of helpful videos that keep everyone on the same page. Embrace this change, and watch your team's productivity and knowledge-sharing improve.

Case Study

Company Overview

One of our clients, a mid-sized automotive parts manufacturer, faced high staff turnover in its Accounts department, making training a recurring challenge. Traditional, text-heavy SOPs were slow to teach the new team members and quite a task to update whenever there was a change in the process.

Challenge

New hires struggled with the steep learning curve brought on by outdated and complex SOPs, leading to significant operational delays and increased error rates.

Implementation of Video SOPs

To address these issues, the company introduced Video SOPs, leveraging screen recordings of accounting and compliance processes like invoice processing, tax filings, and account reconciliations. These recordings were made using Zoom, where experienced employees detailed each action and its purpose through shorter-duration videos. These videos were hosted in the google drive with an index file to search the relevant video with a hyperlink.

Results

The shift to Video SOPs reduced training time by 47%, allowing new hires to understand procedures quickly and accurately.

● ● ● ●

Chapter 2

Mastering Assessment Readiness

Imagine it's a busy day at the office, and you're focused on aligning the quarterly financials with projections. Suddenly, you're informed that tax authorities want to conduct an assessment... for a financial year that ended three years ago. The team member who handled those accounts has moved on, leaving you to sift through years of data. Your current workload doesn't stop as you scramble to catch up with the past.

This scenario is all too familiar for many finance teams. Revisiting financial data from years ago is a daunting task, disrupting current projects and increasing stress levels.

Flipping the Script with Assessment Readiness

Assessment readiness is your proactive defence. It involves preparing for future tax assessments as soon as you close your books and complete your audit. Why then? Because all the necessary information is fresh and readily available. This foresight simplifies future assessments because tax authorities typically request predictable documents and information.

How to Implement Assessment Readiness

Right after completing your audit, collaborate with your team to predict potential document requests in future assessments. Collect these documents—invoices, contracts, financial statements, and relevant correspondence—and organize them in an accessible digital format. This acts like a time capsule, ensuring that anyone on your team can retrieve and understand the information, regardless of their involvement in the original transactions.

The Payoff

The biggest and most immediate benefit is peace of mind. When tax assessments arise for past years, you're prepared, not panicked. This readiness prevents tax demands due to missing or incomplete information and ensures continuity in your workflows, even as team members change. This strategy isn't just about easing tax assessments; it's about protecting your team's time, reducing stress, and maintaining an accurate and complete financial history, no matter how much time has passed. It's a simple step taken today that can prevent countless problems tomorrow.

Conclusion

In conclusion, mastering assessment readiness is all about being proactive and prepared for future tax assessments before they happen. By organizing key documents, storing them digitally, and keeping records updated, you can save time, reduce stress, and avoid costly mistakes. This simple approach ensures your team can handle assessments smoothly, even when key members leave, keeping your financial operations efficient and hassle-free.

Case study

Challenge

During the Financial Year 2019-20, an EPC contractor struggled with missing documents and high employee turnover in the tax function, complicating tax assessments and leading to knowledge gaps. This led to additional tax demand and high consultancy fee by their tax consultants.

Solution

We helped the company to implement the proactive strategy of assessment readiness during Financial Year 2020-21 in the following ways:

- ***Document Organization:*** *Essential documents, such as contracts and financial statements, were compiled and organized immediately after audits.*
- ***Digital Storage:*** *All records were digitized and stored for easy access, allowing any team member to retrieve necessary documents efficiently.*
- ***Regular Updates:*** *The document system was updated quarterly to maintain current and comprehensive records.*

Results

The readiness strategy paid off during the FY 2020-21 tax assessment:

- ***Efficient Process:*** *Despite a key team member's departure, the tax assessment proceeded without any issues related to document availability.*
- ***Reduced Costs:*** *Organized and accessible documents decreased the need for extensive consultant hours, lowering consultancy fees.*
- ***Less Stress:*** *The system reduced the typical stress associated with tax assessments, allowing the financial team to focus on their core responsibilities.*

●●●●

Chapter 3

The Power of Changing Roles

Ever seen those detective shows where the person handling cash and banking for years gets caught skimming money? These plotlines are not just for TV; they reflect a real risk in accounting and compliance. Allowing someone to remain in a sensitive role for an extended period can sometimes lead to misconduct.

The Risk of Comfort

Prolonged tenure in sensitive positions can breed not just contempt but complacency or even temptation. Post-fraud investigations often reveal that extended durations in these roles make it easier for individuals to rationalize their wrongful actions. This comfort might foster unethical behavior, stressing the importance of monitoring in personnel management.

The Magic of Role Swapping

Role swapping might seem logistically challenging, but it brings significant benefits. Firstly, it prevents individuals from becoming too entrenched in their roles. Fresh eyes can lead to questioning established processes and improving them, fostering innovation within the team. Furthermore, this method allows personnel to get a thorough awareness of the organization's operations, resulting in a more adaptable workforce.

Building a Safety Net

Life's unpredictability—such as illness or sudden departures—makes it essential to have versatile team members ready to step into key roles seamlessly. This not only enhances the team's operational resilience but also ensures a broad skill set across the team, reducing dependence on any single individual and increasing overall organizational stability.

Learning from Other Industries

In industries like banking or retail, routine role changes are standard practice to minimize fraud risk and prevent any one person from becoming too comfortable in a potentially corruptible position. By adopting similar strategies, accounting and compliance teams can proactively safeguard their processes against potential misconduct.

Beyond the Basics

The benefits of changing roles extend beyond security. This practice promotes a flexible, collaborative culture, enhances mutual understanding, and broadens everyone's skill sets, leading to a more cohesive and innovative team environment. Moreover, it encourages open communication and fosters a sense of shared responsibility among team members.

Conclusion

Integrating regular role changes into your team's routine can seem daunting, but it offers substantial benefits—from enhancing processes and preventing fraud to boosting team resilience and skill diversity. Embracing this change can safeguard against risks and drive continuous improvement and innovation. By taking inspiration from industries that prioritize role fluidity, we can cultivate a dynamic approach to team roles that not only protects our organization but also empowers our people to thrive.

● ● ● ●

Chapter 4

Grounding Finance in Reality

Imagine the Finance & Accounts department as a vast sea where streams from every part of the business come together, carrying bits of the company's operations in monetary terms. Yet, despite their central role, finance professionals often feel detached from the day-to-day realities of the business.

The Gap

There is a clear disconnect between the numbers on paper and the real-world activities that generate them. Finance professionals are proficient at managing ledgers and balance sheets, but they may not have a clear understanding of the business processes behind those numbers. Knowing that material costs are rising is different from understanding the reasons firsthand, such as observing the manufacturing process or challenges on the retail floor.

Bridging the Divide

For manufacturing, imagine the insights finance team members could gain from walking the factory floor, seeing the machinery, and understanding the hard work that goes into each product. This first-hand experience can transform their perspective on financial figures, linking every rupee spent or earned to the actual efforts and decisions made in production. Being part of the team can also help finance professionals appreciate the effort involved.

In retail, when finance team members work on the sales floor, they can see how customers interact and what drives sales. This experience gives them better context for the numbers they see in reports, helping them make more informed financial decisions that match what's really happening in the store.

The Joy of Understanding

Understanding the full story behind the numbers brings satisfaction. It makes the work of finance professionals more meaningful and helps them feel connected to the company's mission. When finance teams know the "why" behind the data, their analyses become more relevant and useful.

Smoothing Out Frictions

This approach also reduces friction between finance and other departments. Experiencing the challenges of different teams fosters empathy and mutual respect, breaking down barriers and building a cohesive workplace culture. Improved teamwork leads to better problem-solving and innovation, making the whole organization more agile.

A Walk in Their Shoes

An effective strategy could involve temporarily deputing finance team members to other departments. This immersion allows them to participate in daily operations, providing a ground-up understanding and supporting them with their financial expertise. A finance professional involved in procurement or sales strategy, with first-hand operational knowledge, can offer invaluable insights that help improve decisions and use resources better.

Conclusion

Bringing the Finance and Accounts team closer to the ground realities of the business not only makes their work better but also enriches their overall work experience, fostering a deeper sense of belonging and contribution to the company's mission. It turns numbers into stories, expenses into experiences, and friction into collaboration, building not just a stronger finance team but a more united and resilient business.

Case Study

A mid-sized retail company faced ongoing challenges with its finance team's disconnection from the actual sales operations. The finance team's understanding of daily sales dynamics was limited to numbers on spreadsheets, making it difficult for them to appreciate the operational challenges and customer engagement strategies in play.

Problem

The finance team's detachment led to frequent misunderstandings and frictions with the sales department. Budget allocations, expense approvals, and financial forecasts often did not align with on-ground realities, leading to tensions and inefficiencies.

Solution

The company initiated a novel program where finance team members were assigned to spend time on the retail floor. The initiative aimed to provide the finance professionals with first-hand experience of the sales process, customer interactions, and the operational challenges faced by the sales team.

Results

- ***Improved Understanding:*** *Finance team members gained a deeper appreciation for the challenges and complexities of the retail environment. This experience translated into more realistic budgeting, where financial plans were more closely aligned with actual sales trends and operational needs.*
- ***Enhanced Collaboration:*** *The first-hand exposure helped reduce previous frictions between the sales and finance departments. Finance professionals began to see the sales reports not just as numbers but as outcomes of real-world interactions and efforts.*
- ***Informed Decision-Making:*** *Armed with practical insights from the sales floor, the finance team improved their expense management strategies and became better equipped to handle financial forecasting and variance analysis.*

Chapter 5

Navigating Through Quarters - The Art of Setting Team Goals

In the dynamic world of finance and accounting, where urgent tasks often overshadow important ones, setting quarterly goals is crucial. It's not just about keeping operations running smoothly; it's about steering your team in the right direction and ensuring everyone is united with a common purpose.

Why Quarterly Goals?

Quarterly goals act as a compass, helping prioritize critical projects so they don't get lost amidst daily pressures. These goals should be actionable and strategic, directly contributing to both the team's and the company's broader objectives. For example, include updating Standard Operating Procedures (SOPs), automating manual processes, or reducing monthly book closure times.

The Quarterly Plan: A Blueprint for Success

Imagine starting each quarter with a clear plan that motivates the team towards growth, efficiency, and innovation. This plan should be detailed in a way that integrates seamlessly into daily work, avoiding being sidelined or forgotten.

The Meeting That Matters

The quarterly planning meeting is crucial. Envision a lively session where each team member shares their past achievements and future targets through engaging presentations. This meeting celebrates successes, reviews challenges, and sets the stage for future goals, fostering a culture of accountability and collaboration. Encourage open dialogue during these meetings, allowing team members to voice their ideas and concerns, which can lead to valuable insights and a stronger team bond.

A Leadership Litmus Test

These sessions also serve as a platform for identifying emerging leaders. How individuals set and achieve their goals offers insights into their potential for increased responsibilities and promotions.

Aligning Goals with the Company's Vision

It's vital that individual goals support the broader company objectives, ensuring that each team member's efforts contribute to the overall business success. This alignment helps propel the entire organization towards its long-term goals.

Conclusion

Setting quarterly goals transforms routine tasks into steps towards significant achievements. This practice instils a sense of purpose and cohesion, making each quarter a stepping stone to greater success. As you plan for the next quarter, consider how each goal fits into the larger narrative of your company's journey. Remember, the journey of a thousand miles begins with a single step, and with clear quarterly goals, your team is well-equipped to navigate the path ahead.

Case Study

One of our clients, is a mid-sized manufacturing company, consistently faced challenges to drive improvementrelated projects. Despite the urgent need for operational improvements, significant projects, such as the implementation of a new ERP system, were continually delayed.

When I suggested to the CFO about setting priorities through quarterly goal setting, he was initially reluctant due to concerns about adding to the team's workload, but then decided to give it a try. The objective was to prioritize key tasks and foster a more organized approach to tackling both routine responsibilities and strategic projects.

Results

- ***Direction and Focus:*** *The new practice gave the team clear direction, helping them prioritize and efficiently manage their workload. Previously sidelined projects received the attention they needed.*
- ***Completion of Pending Tasks:*** *Several important tasks that had been pending, including critical financial analyses and compliance updates, were completed. This progress was directly linked to the clear goals and deadlines set at the beginning of each quarter.*
- ***Successful ERP Implementation:*** *One of the major achievements facilitated by this new practice was the successful implementation of Phase-1 of NetSuite ERP system. This project had been postponed several times in the past due to prioritization issues and resource allocation. With the new goal-setting practice, the team was able to dedicate necessary resources and focus to this project, leading to its successful completion.*
- ***Team Empowerment and Morale:*** *The clear goals and recognition system boosted team morale. Members felt more empowered and accountable, which contributed to a more positive work environment and enhanced productivity.*

Chapter 6

Integrating Team Building into Daily Activities

Gone are the days when team building was limited to extravagant annual retreats or obligatory team dinners. It's time to transform team building into a proactive, integral part of daily work life, moving beyond grand events to weave team bonding into everyday interactions.

Everyday Team Building

Effective team building doesn't depend on large budgets or grand gestures. Instead, it grows from small, daily interactions that foster trust, understanding, and camaraderie. Here are practical ways to integrate team building into everyday routines:

- ***Lunch Lotteries:*** Host weekly lunch lotteries where team members pair up randomly for lunch, encouraging personal connections beyond work-related topics. This simple activity encourages personal connections beyond work, helping team members get to know each other better.
- ***Family Days at Work:*** Invite employees' families to the office occasionally. This helps team members see each other more holistically, strengthening interpersonal relationships.
- ***Community Service:*** Engage in community service activities that resonate with your team's values, enhancing a sense of shared purpose and team pride, bringing everyone closer together.
- ***Skill-Sharing Sessions:*** Organize monthly sessions where team members can share personal skills or hobbies. These

sessions can uncover hidden talents and foster a deeper connection among team members.

- *Impromptu Dance Gigs and Yoga Sessions:* Incorporate quick dance breaks or short yoga sessions after lunch. These activities can energize the team and add a fun element to the workday, promoting overall well-being.

Why It Matters

These small, proactive steps toward building a team culture yield significant benefits. They enhance a sense of belonging, reduce stress, and encourage open communication, all of which contribute to a more cohesive, motivated, and productive team.

The Power of Everyday Team Building

While the chase for high productivity often overlooks the potential of everyday team building, it's important to remember that a connected and valued team is a tremendous asset. These practices are more than just morale boosters; they are essential for building strong, resilient teams.

Conclusion

Incorporating team building into daily routines isn't a distraction but a means to enhance the work environment, making it more inclusive and supportive. By fostering small, meaningful connections daily, we build a team that not only works well together but also enjoys being together. This approach ensures that team building is a continuous, enriching part of the work experience, shaping stronger teams one day and one shared experience at a time.

●●●●

Chapter 7

The ATM Framework - Accuracy, Timeliness, Measurement

In the world of accounting and compliances, precision and reliability are non-negotiable. One powerful framework that can elevate any accounting or compliance process is the ATM framework—***Accuracy, Timeliness, and Measurement***. This simple yet profound approach serves as the cornerstone for building a highly efficient and trustworthy financial system across industries.

Understanding the ATM Framework

- *Accuracy:* This is fundamental in accounting. Accuracy ensures that every number, report, and forecast is correct, preventing significant discrepancies that could affect business decisions and strategies.
- ***Timeliness:*** Timeliness is crucial in accounting and compliance. Meeting reporting and compliance deadlines is essential as delays can result in penalties, missed opportunities, or damage to reputation.
- *Measurement:* Often the most overlooked component, measurement is what sets apart successful teams. It involves not just tracking performance but also understanding it to improve processes continually.

The Importance of Measurement

Measurement is more than just tracking data; it requires a commitment to tracking and understanding performance deeply. It's about identifying what's working well and where improvements are needed. Effective measurement drives behavior, focusing efforts on what truly impacts performance making it a key element of the ATM framework.

Implementing Measurement Effectively

For measurement to be truly impactful, it should be simple and straightforward. Employing Pareto's law, or the 80/20 rule, helps you focus on the 20% of metrics that deliver 80% of the results, simplifying the process and highlighting the most impactful areas.

Steps to Implement the ATM Framework

1. ***Start with Accuracy:*** Review and refine processes to minimize errors. Implement checks and balances to maintain data integrity. Regular training for team members on the importance of accuracy can also help reduce mistakes.
2. ***Ensure Timeliness:*** Clearly map all deadlines and create a schedule that allows for the completion of tasks ahead of time, including buffers for unexpected delays. Regular progress check-ins can help keep the team on track.
3. ***Master Measurement:*** Select key metrics that reflect your financial processes' health, such as error rates or compliance rates. Focus on these critical metrics, ensure they are understood by the team, and use them to guide improvements.

Impact of the ATM Framework

Adopting the ATM framework commits your team to continuous improvement and excellence. It transforms routine tasks into opportunities for growth and creates a culture where accuracy, timeliness, and measurement are the pillars of work ethic. This approach not only meets but exceeds expectations, turning everyday financial management into a robust, integrity-driven process.

Embracing the ATM framework means measuring, improving, and celebrating successes systematically. It ensures that in the realm of finance, the real value lies not just in monetary transactions but in trust, reliability, and ongoing enhancement of processes.

Conclusion

The ATM framework—Accuracy, Timeliness, and Measurement—is essential for improving financial processes. By focusing on these key areas, teams can reduce errors, meet deadlines, and track performance effectively. This approach not only enhances efficiency but also fosters a culture of continuous improvement, helping organizations make better decisions and build trust. Embracing the ATM framework means creating a stronger foundation for financial success.

Case Study

A manufacturing company's CFO faced significant inefficiencies in financial processes, particularly in vendor invoice processing and management information system (MIS) reporting, alongside poor interdepartmental communication.

Implementation of the ATM Framework

To address these challenges, the CFO implemented the ATM framework – focusing on Accuracy, Timeliness, and Measurement:

- ***Accuracy:*** *New verification steps were introduced along with some automation to eliminate inaccuracies in vendor invoice processing and MIS preparation.*
- ***Timeliness:*** *Specific deadlines were set for all financial processes, especially for the processing of vendor invoices and the generation of MIS reports.*
- ***Measurement:*** *Key Performance Indicators (KPIs) were established to monitor the accuracy and timeliness of financial operations, with regular performance reviews to ensure continuous improvement.*

Results

- ***Vendor Invoice Processing:*** *Processing time was reduced by 37%, enhancing cash flow management and vendor relationships.*
- ***MIS Reporting:*** *MIS reports became more accurate and were consistently prepared on time, aiding in better decision-making.*
- ***Increased Transparency:*** *The new measurement and reporting protocols increased transparency, improving communication and collaboration across departments.*

● ● ● ●

Chapter 8

Mastering Executive Meetings

In the busy world of finance, tasks come and go as quickly as emails on a Monday morning. For CFOs and financial controllers, managing the routine number crunching is just part of the job. The real challenge lies in keeping track of non-recurring tasks that often get sidelined amid daily urgencies.

The Slippery Slope of Non-Recurring Tasks

Let's visualize a common scenario: You've assigned a team member to prepare a one-off report for the Purchasing department or to follow up on vital information from a vendor. Initially, these tasks seem straightforward. However, as days pass and new projects emerge, these "simple" tasks can easily get buried under an avalanche of more pressing emails. It's not limited to just reports or follow-ups. Setting up a new software trial, organizing a tax update training session, or negotiating a new contract are all critical yet sporadic tasks that risk being overlooked. The impact of losing track of these tasks can be significant, leading to missed opportunities, delayed responses, and potential financial discrepancies.

Solution: The Weekly Executive Meeting - A Game Changer

The solution might sound straightforward: a weekly executive meeting with each team member. However, the effectiveness of these meetings lies in their execution:

- ***Transparency Through Google Sheets:*** A shared Google Sheet lists all pending non-recurring tasks, visible to the entire team. This transparency ensures accountability and a bit of healthy pressure. No one wants to be seen as the team member lagging behind.
- ***The Current vs. Remaining System:*** Tasks are categorized as either 'Current' (the focus for the upcoming week) or 'Remaining' (deferred for now). Each team member prioritizes their tasks for the week, clearly marking their commitments.
- ***The End-of-Week Reckoning:*** By Friday, tasks are marked green for 'completed' or red for 'incomplete'. This simple, effective system promotes a brutally honest assessment of each person's weekly achievements.
- ***Monday Meetings:*** Scheduled on Monday to set the week's tone, these meetings review the previous week's successes and failures and align everyone on the week's priorities.
- ***Duration of Meetings:*** Each meeting lasts just 15-30 minutes, focusing on conciseness, focus, and productivity.
- ***The Twist in Scoring:*** If a team member commits to five tasks and completes four, the success rate isn't 80% but rather seen as -20%. It emphasizes the importance of what was not accomplished (to avoid complacency), reinforcing complete accountability.

The Culture Shift

Implementing this weekly system does more than prevent tasks from slipping through the cracks—it cultivates a culture of transparency, accountability, and simplicity. This approach ensures everyone knows what's expected, understands their performance, and sees how they contribute to the team's success. Using Google Sheets, tasks can be added instantly from anywhere, ensuring thorough tracking and accountability.

Conclusion

The weekly executive meeting isn't just a routine check-in; it's a foundational practice that fosters clarity, responsibility, and continual progress. It transforms daunting tasks into manageable actions and chaotic workflows into coordinated efforts. For CFOs and financial controllers aiming to navigate their responsibilities with precision, these meetings are an indispensable tool that can lead to smoother operations and a more engaged team.

Case Study

A multinational company struggled to manage non-recurring tasks in its Finance & Accounts Function amid business diversification, leading to inefficiencies and missed opportunities.

The CFO faced challenges in tracking and completing critical tasks such as contract negotiations, incentive calculation due to change in policy, renewal of insurance policy, filing of appeal against a GST demand order etc. The sporadic nature of these tasks, combined with the daily demands of operations, complicated the situation.

Solution

The CFO introduced a structured approach to enhance task management:

- ***Google Sheets Tracker:** A live document was used to list all non-recurring tasks, categorized as 'Current' or 'Remaining.' This document was visible to all team members, ensuring transparency and real-time updates.*
- ***Weekly Executive Meetings:** Held every Monday for 30 minutes, these meetings reviewed task progress from the previous week and set priorities for the current week, with tasks marked green for completed and red for incomplete to ensure accountability.*

Results

- ***Efficient Task Management:** The tracking system and regular meetings improved the management of non-recurring tasks, allowing for timely completion and better prioritization.*
- ***Increased Operational Efficiency:** The clear weekly focus led to faster execution of tasks.*
- ***Improved Communication:** Regular updates and transparent task statuses enhanced interdepartmental communication, aligning expectations and smoothing workflows across the company.*

Chapter 9

Keeping a Pulse on Progress - Day-End Reporting of Key KPIs

In the bustling world of finance and accounting, staying ahead means keeping a constant pulse on how well the team is performing against their key objectives. This is where the concept of day-end reporting of key KPIs comes into play—a simple yet powerful tool that ensures everyone is on the same page, every single day.

The Essence of KPIs in Finance and Compliance

Key Performance Indicators (KPIs) in accounting and compliance are often the unsung heroes that keep the wheels of finance turning smoothly. However, pinpointing these KPIs and ensuring they're part of the daily conversation is something many companies overlook. The trick is not to overcomplicate things.

The Rule of Five

When it comes to setting daily KPIs, the golden rule is to keep it short and simple. A list longer than five daily KPIs is overkill and can dilute focus rather than sharpen it. The goal is to concentrate on a handful of metrics that truly matter, ensuring they are clear, measurable, and directly linked to the team's and company's broader objectives.

Examples of Daily KPIs

- ***Invoice Tracker Updates:*** Ensuring the invoice tracker is updated daily provides a real-time view of accounts receivable, crucial for managing cash flow.

- ***Email Responsiveness:*** Setting a goal to reply to all emails within a specific timeframe keeps communication channels open and efficient.
- ***Transaction Processing:*** Tracking the number of transactions processed daily helps gauge productivity and identify any backlogs early on.
- ***Compliance Checklist Progress:*** Keeping a daily tab on the progress made on compliance checklists ensures that nothing falls through the cracks, keeping the company on the right side of regulations.
- ***Expense Report Submissions:*** Monitoring the timeliness and accuracy of expense report submissions can prevent reimbursement delays and financial discrepancies.

Simplifying the Reporting Process

The beauty of this system lies in its simplicity. The daily KPI report should be so straightforward that filling it out and sharing it takes no more than five minutes. A simple spreadsheet can serve this purpose, with columns for each KPI and easy color-coded statuses or check marks to indicate completion.

Overcoming the Hurdle of Daily Reporting

The thought of daily reporting might sound daunting to some. Yet, when implemented correctly, it's anything but burdensome. A streamlined reporting process that takes just a couple of minutes at the end of the day ensures that everyone is aware of their progress without the need for time-consuming meetings or follow-ups.

The Power of Daily Insights

The true value of daily KPI reporting is in its ability to keep the team aligned, focused, and aware of their performance in real-time. It's not just about monitoring; it's a proactive approach to management. By investing a few minutes each day, team leaders can stay on top of things effortlessly, fostering a culture of transparency and accountability.

Ideal for Onboarding New Team Members

This approach proves exceptionally beneficial for new team members. It offers a structured way for them to share updates on their work, easing the onboarding process and helping them integrate more smoothly into the team's workflow.

Conclusion

In essence, day-end reporting of key KPIs is more than just a tracking tool; it's a cornerstone of effective team management in the finance and compliance function. By keeping it simple, short, and sweet, you unlock the potential of daily insights, leading to better decision-making, enhanced productivity, and a team that's always aligned with the company's financial goals. So, let's embrace the simplicity and clarity that daily KPI reporting brings to the table, and watch as it transforms the rhythm and results of our finance teams.

Case Study

A mid-sized tech firm faced inefficiencies and unclear task management in its finance department, leading to frequent task delays and high employee turnover.

Problem

The lack of structure in monitoring daily tasks resulted in piling work, missed deadlines, and confusion over responsibilities. Employees often felt overwhelmed and underappreciated, contributing to the high attrition rate.

Introduction of Day-End KPI Reporting

The CFO introduced a simple day-end KPI reporting system where team members tracked key performance indicators (KPIs) related to their daily tasks, such as processing times and accuracy rates.

Results

- ***Increased Efficiency:*** *Task pendency decreased by 37% as team members became more diligent in completing their work on time.*
- ***Enhanced Responsibility:*** *The system provided clarity on individual roles and responsibilities, leading to smoother operations.*
- ***Improved Retention:*** *Employees felt more valued, leading to better job satisfaction and a noticeable improvement in retention rates.*

Conclusion

The introduction of day-end KPI reporting helped the finance department eliminate inefficiencies, increase accountability, and boost employee engagement, ultimately transforming the team's productivity and morale.

● ● ● ●

Chapter 10

Fine-Tuning the Finance Team - A Guide to the Hiring Process

Hiring the right team member in the world of finance and accounting is more than just filling a vacant spot; it's about finding a piece that perfectly fits the puzzle of your team, especially when each member's contribution is vital due to a small team size. Despite its importance, the hiring process in many organizations, particularly in the finance and accounts departments, often lacks the depth and rigor it truly deserves.

The Proven Path to Hiring Excellence

Achieving a good hire isn't about luck; it's about preparation and having a clear understanding of what you're looking for. This clarity comes from asking the right questions—questions that delve into both the technical capabilities and the behavioral traits of your potential team member. Here's why this matters:

- ***Technical questions*** assess the candidate's ability to perform the job's core functions.
- ***Behavioral questions*** reveal how the candidate approaches work, interacts with others, and fits into your company culture.

Crafting Your Interview Arsenal

Creating a comprehensive list of interview questions is an investment in your team's future. It ensures you cover all bases, leaving nothing to assume. Here are examples of questions that should make it to your list, divided into technical and behavioral categories:

Technical Questions:

- ***"How do you stay current with changes in accounting standards and regulations?"*** This question reveals the candidate's commitment to professional growth and their proactive approach to the ever-evolving financial landscape.
- ***"Can you walk me through your process for month-end?"*** Understanding their approach gives insight into their organizational skills and attention to detail.
- ***"Describe a challenging financial analysis you've conducted. What made it challenging, and what was the outcome?"*** This sheds light on their analytical thinking and problem-solving abilities.
- ***"How would you handle discovering a significant reporting error?"*** This explores their integrity and approach to problem resolution.

Behavioral Questions

- ***"Tell me about a time when you had to work under tight deadlines.*** How did you manage your workload?" This question assesses time management skills and ability to work under pressure.
- ***"Describe a situation where you had a disagreement with a team member. How was it resolved?"*** This explores their conflict resolution skills and ability to work as part of a team.
- ***"Give an example of a goal you failed to achieve. What did you learn from it?"*** Understanding their response to setbacks can provide insight into their resilience and capacity for growth.
- "How do you prioritize your tasks when everything seems urgent?" This question reveals their decision-making process and ability to manage priorities.

The Importance of Being Specific

Vagueness is the enemy of a good hire. Specificity in your questions not only helps you get to know the candidate better but also sets clear expectations for what the role entails. Remember, the goal is to understand not just if they can do the job, but how they will do the job and interact with your team.

The Long-Term Benefits

Investing time upfront in creating a solid list of interview questions pays off manifold. It not only saves the time and resources that go into training a misfit and potentially restarting the hiring process but also serves as a valuable tool for future vacancies. Having a ready set of questions ensures consistency in your hiring process and helps in building a strong, cohesive team over time.

Conclusion

In the quest for the perfect finance and accounts team member, the depth of your interview process can make all the difference. By blending technical and behavioral inquiries, you're not just filling a position; you're investing in the future success of your team. So, take the time to craft those questions. Your future self—and your team—will thank you.

● ● ● ●

Chapter 11

Cultivating Growth - Training and Development in Finance and Accounting

In the bustling corridors of finance and accounting, where the clock never seems to tick slowly enough, the concept of training and development often becomes a wishlist item—much talked about but rarely acted upon. Every CFO knows the value of elevating their team's skills, yet the reality of tight schedules and pressing deadlines can make this crucial aspect take a backseat. However, overlooking training and development is akin to ignoring the fuel that keeps the engine of your team running at its peak. Just as a well-maintained engine drives efficiency, a well-trained team drives success.

The Win-Win of Continuous Learning

Investing in the growth of your team is not just a nice-to-have; it's a strategic move. A well-trained team is more efficient, more capable, and more motivated. The trick lies in integrating training into the DNA of your daily operations, making it as routine as checking emails or attending meetings. When training becomes part of the daily workflow, it ensures that every team member is equipped with the latest skills and knowledge needed to excel.

The Magic of Compounding in Training

Let's talk about Excel. In finance and accounting, Excel isn't just a tool; it's the lifeblood. Imagine introducing a routine where your team dedicates just 15 minutes a day to an advanced Excel online course. These bite-sized learning sessions may seem brief, but over a month, they add up to approximately five hours of specialized training. This approach demonstrates the magic of compounding—small, consistent efforts lead to significant growth over time.

Saturday Sessions: Learning and Sharing

Why not turn one of the quieter days in the office into a dedicated learning day? Pick a Saturday or any other less hectic day, and initiate a tradition where team members take turns delivering a short presentation on a topic of their choice. Limiting the presentation to under 10 slides and 30 minutes encourages concise communication and respects everyone's time. This not only sharpens presentation skills but also fosters a culture of sharing knowledge and expertise, particularly encouraging for younger team members eager to showcase their insights. By creating this platform, you empower everyone to learn from one another, enriching the entire team's expertise.

Monthly Behavioral Skills Boost

Technical skills are just one side of the coin; behavioral skills are equally important, especially in a field as collaborative as finance and accounting. Organizing a monthly 30-minute session focused on soft skills—from effective communication and teamwork to leadership and time management—can significantly enhance the interpersonal dynamics of your team. This regular investment in behavioral training can lead to a more harmonious and productive workplace.

Other Creative Training Avenues

- ***Book Clubs:*** Launch a monthly book club focusing on both technical finance topics and broader business or personal development books. This initiative encourages continuous learning and sparks insightful discussions among team members.

- ***Finance Fridays:*** Dedicate one Friday each month to exploring new financial software, tools, or technologies. Keeping abreast of the latest digital advancements ensures your team remains at the forefront of the industry.
- ***Peer-to-Peer Coaching:*** Pair up team members with different strengths for mutual coaching sessions. This peer-to-peer approach leverages the diverse skill sets within your team, promoting a culture of mutual growth and support.
- ***Industry Webinars:*** Encourage team members to attend online webinars and workshops relevant to your industry. Allocating time for these activities during work hours underscores your commitment to their professional development.

Conclusion

Incorporating training and development into the routine of your finance and accounting team is not just beneficial; it's essential for staying competitive and maintaining a high level of job satisfaction among your team members. By embracing creative and manageable ways to foster continuous learning, you're not only investing in the individual growth of your team members but also enhancing the collective capability and efficiency of your team as a whole. Remember, the most successful teams are those that grow together, learn together, and succeed together.

● ● ● ●

Chapter 12

The Benchmarking Blueprint

In finance and accounting, stagnation is not a viable choice. The key to success lies in continuous improvement, but how can we measure our progress? This is where benchmarking steps in—it serves as our guiding light amid the sea of data and reports, steering us toward achieving excellence.

The Essence of Benchmarking

At its core, benchmarking is about setting a standard, a target to aim for. Without a benchmark, improvement is like shooting arrows in the dark, hoping to hit a target we can't see. Benchmarks can come from outside the company (external) or be developed within (internal). While grabbing those external benchmarks can be tricky, relying solely on internal ones might keep us playing it safe within our comfort zone.

The Two Faces of Benchmarking

External benchmarks offer us a glimpse into how we stack up against the industry at large. They pull us out of our bubble and expose us to the broader playing field. However, getting hold of this data often requires some work, such as diving into industry reports, or joining benchmarking groups.

Internal benchmarks, on the other hand, are more accessible. They're about competing against ourselves, striving to do better today than we did yesterday. But here's the catch: if we're not ambitious enough, we might just end up celebrating mediocrity, patting ourselves on the back for jumping over low bars.

Benchmarking in Action: Examples to Aim For

- ***Cost of Finance & Accounts Function as a % of Revenue:*** This varies by industry, but a common target falls between 0.75% and 1.5% of total revenue. It's a metric that forces us to look at efficiency and scalability side by side.
- ***Transactions Per Team Member:*** When it comes to tasks like vendor invoice processing, how many transactions can a team member handle? Setting a benchmark here pushes for productivity and process improvements.
- ***Monthly Close:*** The race to close the books each month. A clear deadline not only keeps the team on their toes but also ensures timely reporting and analysis.
- ***Statutory Audit Deadlines:*** Marking the calendar for when the audit needs to be wrapped up encourages planning and coordination, making sure no one's burning the midnight oil at the last minute.
- ***Days Sales Outstanding (DSO):*** This measures how quickly revenue turns into cash. A tighter DSO range means better cash flow management.
- ***Inventory Levels:*** Especially critical for product-based businesses, benchmarking inventory levels against sales ensures capital isn't tied up unnecessarily.

The Power of Benchmarking

Benchmarking isn't just about setting targets; it's about stretching the limits of what we think is possible. It brings a sense of urgency, a push towards optimization and efficiency that can transform the finance function from a cost center to a value driver.

Moreover, when teams see what's being achieved elsewhere, it ignites a drive to not just meet but exceed those standards. It's about creating a culture where "good enough" never is, where the status quo is always questioned, and where continuous improvement is part of the daily routine.

Cultivating a Benchmarking Culture

To truly embed benchmarking in the fabric of our operations, it must become more than an occasional exercise. It requires:

- ***Regular Reviews:*** Making benchmarking a regular part of performance discussions keeps everyone aligned and focused on the targets.
- ***Transparency:*** Sharing benchmarks and progress openly fosters a culture of accountability and collective effort.
- ***Celebrating Wins:*** Recognizing when benchmarks are met or exceeded can boost morale and motivation across the team.

Conclusion

Benchmarking is our roadmap to excellence, a tool that sharpens our focus and guides our efforts. By embracing both internal and external benchmarks, we not only set our sights on what's achievable but also challenge ourselves to redefine the boundaries of possibility. Let's not just aim to meet benchmarks; let's strive to set new ones, driving our team, our department, and our company to new heights of performance and efficiency.

● ● ● ●

Chapter 13

Mastering Your Most Valuable Asset - Time

In the high-stakes world of finance, where decisions can change markets and shape futures, the Chief Financial Officer (CFO) stands as the guardian of not just the company's fiscal health but also its strategic direction. Among all the responsibilities, there's one asset more precious than the most bullish stock or the most stable currency: time. Time can be either spent or invested, and the return on investment (ROI) on time well invested is unparalleled.

The Surprising Reality of Time Management for CFOs

If you ask any CFO where their time goes, they will confidently list tasks, meetings, and strategic initiatives. However, when they start tracking their actual time, a startling revelation unfolds: the majority of CFOs find a significant disconnect between their perceived time expenditure and reality. This isn't for a lack of expertise or intention but rather a reflection of the complex, often reactive nature of the role.

Facing the Music: The Challenge of Self-Monitoring

Admitting the need to track one's time is the first step in conquering this challenge. It's not an easy task. There's a certain vulnerability in facing the reality of how our hours are spent, especially when intuition tells us one thing, and the data reveals another. This resistance isn't just about confronting inefficiencies; it's about challenging our own narrative of productivity and purpose.

My Personal Journey with Time Tracking

Since the inception of Blue Consulting Pvt. Ltd. in 2005, maintaining a daily timesheet has evolved from a simple experiment into a cornerstone of my professional routine. At first, the idea of logging every hour seemed daunting, perhaps even a bit obsessive. However, over time, this practice has shown me not just where my hours are going but also where they should be going. It has given me invaluable insights into my own working habits, priorities, and, importantly, areas for improvement.

How to Start Tracking Your Time

The beauty of time tracking lies in its simplicity. You don't need sophisticated software or complex systems. A straightforward Google Sheet can serve as your canvas, offering both accessibility and flexibility. Here's a simple format to get started:

- Date
- Task
- Time Spent
- Category (Strategic Planning, Operational Tasks, Meetings, etc.)

The key is consistency. Make it a habit to log your activities, however mundane they might seem. The act of tracking isn't just about accountability; it's about gaining clarity and making informed decisions on reallocating your most limited resource.

The Benefits Unveiled

Beyond the initial revelation of how time is spent, this practice brings several additional benefits:

- ***Prioritization:*** Identifying time sinks allows for a reallocation of effort towards high-impact activities.

- ***Delegation:*** Recognizing tasks that can be delegated frees up space for strategic thinking and leadership.
- ***Efficiency:*** Over time, patterns emerge, highlighting opportunities to streamline processes and reduce wasted effort.
- ***Balance:*** Tracking time can also shine a light on the work-life balance, or often, the lack thereof, prompting necessary adjustments.

Conclusion

For CFOs and finance leaders navigating the complexities of modern business, mastering time management through diligent tracking is not just a practice but a necessity. It transforms time from a fleeting resource into a strategic asset, one that, when invested wisely, yields dividends in productivity, clarity, and overall satisfaction. So, take the leap, start logging those hours, and watch as the once elusive asset of time becomes your most reliable ally in the quest for personal and professional excellence.

Chapter 14

Embracing Automation - A Practical Guide for CFOs

In the current business landscape, the word "automation" has almost become a cliché, popping up in every other conversation in the corporate world. For CFOs, the pressure to stay on top of this trend can be overwhelming, especially with the constant buzz around artificial intelligence (AI) and its impact on business processes.

Automation: The Hype and the Reality

It's hard to escape the hype. From media discussions to boardroom debates, automation seems to be the silver bullet for achieving efficiency and control. As a CFO, you might feel the push to jump on the bandwagon quickly. But here's the thing: automation is not just a trendy project to tick off the list; it's a strategic journey that requires careful thought and planning.

The Automation Journey: Start with Standardization

Before diving into the technicalities, it's crucial to understand that effective automation begins with standardization. You can't automate a process that isn't consistent or well-defined. Standardizing processes ensures that they are repeatable and predictable, making them suitable for automation. Without this foundational step, any attempt at automation can lead to chaos, resulting in wasted resources and potential setbacks.

Learning the Ropes

Given the complexities and constantly changing nature of automation technologies, it's wise for CFOs to get their hands dirty with some basic learning. There are numerous online courses available on automation that can provide a solid foundation in understanding how these technologies can be tailored specifically to finance and accounting functions. This knowledge not only helps in making informed decisions but also in leading automation initiatives more effectively.

Key Factors for Successful Automation

When embarking on the automation journey, three critical factors come into play:

1. ***Clarity of Purpose:*** Know exactly what you want to achieve with automation. Is it reducing the time spent on data entry? Enhancing the accuracy of financial reports? Streamlining compliance processes? Having specific goals sets the direction for your automation efforts and ensures that you remain focused on achieving meaningful results.
2. ***Adaptation:*** The ability to adapt is crucial. Automation may require shifts in workflow, roles, and responsibilities. Being flexible and open to change can significantly smooth these transitions.
3. ***Leadership Involvement:*** Successful automation projects often have one thing in common—active involvement from senior leaders. When leaders are engaged, it sends a message that the project is a priority, fostering a culture of acceptance and cooperation across the team.

Starting Small: Practical Automation Initiatives

For CFOs looking to introduce automation, it's advisable to start with small, manageable projects that deliver quick wins.

Here are some practical examples:

- ***Automating Data Extraction:*** Implement tools that automatically extract data from emails and documents, reducing the need for manual entry and freeing up time for more strategic tasks.
- ***Compiling Reports:*** Use automation to gather data from various sources into a single report. This not only saves time but also ensures accuracy.
- ***Reconciliation Processes:*** Automate the reconciliation of accounts to speed up month-end close processes and reduce errors.
- ***Automating Invoice Processing:*** Tools can automatically capture and process information from invoices, streamlining accounts payable.
- ***Regular Compliance Checks:*** Set up systems to automatically run checks for compliance requirements, ensuring that nothing is missed and reducing the risk of penalties.

Conclusion

As a CFO, embracing automation doesn't mean overhauling all your processes overnight. It's about thoughtful implementation, starting with the basics and gradually scaling up. By choosing the right projects, investing in learning, and involving your team at every step, you can harness the power of automation to enhance efficiency, accuracy, and ultimately elevate the strategic impact of your finance department. Remember, automation is a journey—an exciting one that holds the promise of transforming not just your operations but also your role as a CFO.

Case Study

A large retail company faced challenges with its manual and inconsistent accounts payable process, which led to inefficiencies and vendor dissatisfaction.

Problem

The accounts payable process was slow and error-prone, negatively affecting financial operations and relationships with vendors.

Solution

Automation via RPA and Standardization: The CFO spearheaded a project to standardize and automate the accounts payable process using Robotic Process Automation (RPA).

- ***Standardization:** Clear procedures for invoice handling, from submission to payment, were established to ensure consistency across all departments.*
- ***RPA Implementation:** RPA technology was adopted to automate invoice data capture, validation, and payment processing, focusing on adaptation rather than extensive customization. This approach reduced the implementation time by 30%.*

KPI Monitoring:

KPIs were introduced to monitor improvements, such as processing time per invoice and error rates in payments.

Results

- ***Increased Efficiency:** The automation led to a 43% reduction in processing time per invoice, enhancing vendor relations.*
- ***Improved Accuracy:** RPA minimized errors in data entry and calculations, leading to more accurate financial reporting.*
- ***Higher Employee Retention:** Reducing manual tasks allowed employees to focus on more strategic activities, improving job satisfaction and retention rates.*

Conclusion

The integration of RPA after standardizing processes significantly streamlined the accounts' payable function, demonstrating the value of aligning technological enhancements with prepared operational standards. This strategic approach not only optimized workflows but also strengthened the finance team's role within the broader business context.

●●●●

Chapter 15

The Power of Checklists in Finance and Accounting

In an age where AI and high-tech solutions dominate discussions in corporate circles, the humble checklist might seem like a relic from a simpler time. But don't be fooled. As Atul Gawande illustrates in his influential book, The Checklist Manifesto, this simple tool holds transformative powers, enabling precision and consistency across various high-stakes fields, including healthcare, aviation, and, yes, finance and accounting.

Checklists: Your Defense Against the Complexities of Finance

The modern CFO faces a complex array of responsibilities, from regulatory compliance and risk management to financial reporting and strategic planning. Each of these areas contains a multitude of detailed processes that can overwhelm even the most seasoned professionals. This is where checklists come into their own, turning complexity into manageable, actionable tasks.

The Crucial Role of Checklists in Managing Complexity

- *Simplifying Complexity:* Finance and accounting are filled with complex procedures that can be daunting to even the most experienced professionals. A well-designed checklist breaks these down into simpler, doable steps, ensuring that all critical actions are taken.

- ***Catching Errors:*** The smallest oversight in finance can lead to significant problems. Checklists act as a fail-safe, catching errors before they escalate into costly mistakes.
- ***Promoting Standardization:*** Consistency is key in financial operations. Checklists ensure that every process, whether it's closing the books monthly or annual tax returns, is performed the same way every time, reducing variability and enhancing reliability.
- ***Facilitating Communication:*** In finance teams, where tasks are often interdependent, checklists clarify who is responsible for what and by when. This transparency improves teamwork and efficiency.
- ***Instilling Discipline:*** Routine might not sound exciting, but it's the backbone of effective finance management. Checklists enforce a disciplined approach to daily tasks, ensuring nothing is missed even on the busiest days.
- ***Empowering Teams:*** By outlining clear steps and expectations, checklists empower team members to complete tasks with confidence. They know exactly what needs to be done, reducing hesitation and the need for constant supervision.

The Two Types of Checklists: Preventive and Detective

- ***Checklists come in two flavors:*** preventive and detective. Both are valuable, but their applications differ:
- ***Preventive Checklists:*** These are designed to prevent errors before they occur. For example, a pre-payment audit checklist ensures that all invoices are verified and approved before payments are processed, preventing fraud or payment errors.
- ***Detective Checklists:*** These help in identifying issues that have already occurred but are not yet apparent. For example, a monthly reconciliation checklist helps in spotting discrepancies in accounts before they affect the financial statements.

Practical Applications in Finance and Accounting

Implementing checklists can revolutionize the efficiency and accuracy of financial operations. Here are some areas where CFOs can integrate checklists:

- ***Monthly and Year-End Close:*** Ensure that all necessary journal entries are made, and accounts are reconciled accurately.
- ***Payroll Processing:*** Verify that all employee data is updated and accurate before processing payroll.
- ***Tax Returns:*** Check that all deductions are accounted for and that returns are compliant with current tax laws.
- ***Complex Reconciliations:*** Regularly check for discrepancies in major accounts, such as inventory or receivables.
- ***Onboarding Vendors and Customers:*** Verify all required documents and information are collected and recorded accurately.

Personal and Team Empowerment Through Checklists

On a personal note, the effectiveness of checklists isn't limited to professional tasks. For example, I've used a vacation checklist to ensure my family and I don't forget essentials that could impact our enjoyment of a trip. This same principle applies to daily operations in a finance department—checklists ensure everything needed for efficient workflow is ready and accounted for.

Conclusion

In conclusion, the modest checklist is a powerful tool in the arsenal of any CFO. Far from being outdated, it is a testament to how simple tools can provide solutions to complex problems, ensuring accuracy, promoting efficiency, and maintaining compliance in the fast-paced world of finance. Whether preventive or detective, these checklists not only safeguard the financial health of an organization but also enhance the strategic role of finance in overall business success.

Case study

A financial services firm faced persistent errors in accounting and compliance, undermining trust in financial reports and consuming substantial managerial time.

Problem

Frequent errors in financial processes diminished data reliability and demanded excessive intervention from the CFO and senior finance staff.

Solution

Implementation of Checklists: The CFO introduced detailed checklists for key financial operations including monthly closings, payroll, and tax returns to prevent errors and streamline tasks.

- ***Checklist Development:*** *Targeted checklists were developed for essential financial procedures to ensure accuracy and completeness.*
- ***Training and Implementation:*** *Staff were trained on checklist usage integrated into the financial system, guiding them through each step of critical processes.*

Results

- ***Reduction in Errors:*** *The implementation of checklists led to a remarkable 73% decrease in errors, significantly bolstering the reliability of financial data.*
- ***Increased Trust and Efficiency:*** *Greater data accuracy boosted stakeholder trust and freed up senior management to focus on strategic initiatives rather than daily issues.*
- ***Improved Retention:*** *Clearer processes increased job satisfaction, enhancing employee retention within the finance team.*

Conclusion

The strategic use of checklists markedly improved the accuracy and efficiency of financial operations, proving their value in modern financial management by reducing errors, enhancing data reliability, and freeing up managerial bandwidth.

● ● ● ●

Chapter 16

From Accountant to Business Accountant - Elevating the Finance Function

Transforming an accountant into a business accountant is an ambitious endeavor—it's easier said than done, but the rewards are worth it. Typically, the role of accountants in a company is viewed through a narrow lens, focused primarily on crunching numbers, managing ledgers, and ensuring compliance. But what if we could broaden that view?

Understanding the Traditional Accountant Mindset

Most accountants are trained to be highly efficient in specific tasks: processing transactions, ensuring accurate bookkeeping, and adhering to compliance requirements. Their world revolves around debits, credits, and tax regulations—essential elements, no doubt. But often, this focus is so intense that it doesn't leave room for anything else.

The Need for a Shift

However, the Finance & Accounts department holds a unique position within a company. It can see what happens in all departments because every part of a business ultimately affects profits or expenses. This puts accountants in a perfect position to not just report on numbers but to understand and influence the broader business dynamics that those numbers reflect.

What Makes a Business Accountant?

A business accountant is a step beyond the traditional role. While a typical accountant might ask, "Is this transaction recorded correctly?", a business accountant will also consider, "How does this transaction impact our business objectives?". Here are some key differences:

- ***Strategic Thinking:*** Unlike traditional accountants who may focus solely on accuracy and compliance, business accountants think strategically about financial management. They understand how financial decisions impact various parts of the business and contribute to long-term goals.
- ***Proactive Insights:*** Instead of just recording financial history, business accountants analyze data to provide insights that inform future business strategies. They play a crucial role in forecasting and planning, helping steer the company towards its financial targets.
- ***Cross-Functional Collaboration:*** Business accountants work closely with other departments, providing financial insights that help marketing, sales, and production teams make more informed decisions. Their work is integral to solving business problems, not just accounting problems.
- ***Value Addition:*** The transition from an accountant to a business accountant means moving from repetitive tasks to dynamic involvement in business growth. This shift not only enhances the value they bring to the organization but also significantly boosts their career trajectory.

Training and Development: The Pathway to Change

Achieving this transformation requires more than just a change in job description. It involves a comprehensive shift in training and mindset:

- ***Educational Workshops:*** Regular training sessions that not only update accountants on the latest in compliance and financial regulations but also on business strategy and market trends.

- ***Mentorship Programs:*** Pairing accountants with business leaders within the company can provide them with insights into the strategic decision-making process and broaden their understanding of the business as a whole.
- ***Cross-Departmental Projects:*** Involving accountants in projects beyond the finance department can help them see firsthand how their work affects and is affected by other parts of the business.
- ***Analytics Training:*** Since data is at the core of strategic business decisions, equipping accountants with skills in data analysis and interpretation is crucial. This might include training in advanced Excel, data visualization tools, or even introductory courses in business analytics.

Conclusion

Transforming traditional accountants into business accountants is not just about adding new skills but about redefining their role within the company. By expanding their view from the ledger to the entire landscape of the business, accountants can evolve into strategic partners who not only understand the financial implications of business decisions but also influence them. This transformation not only benefits the individual by enhancing their career prospects and job satisfaction but also drives the company forward by integrating financial intelligence into every aspect of its operations.

● ● ● ●

Chapter 17

A Comprehensive Approach to Monthly Closing - Beyond the Profit and Loss

In the rush of monthly financial closures, many companies tend to focus heavily on the Profit and Loss (P&L) statement. It's understandable—after all, the P&L provides a clear view of the financial performance for the month, tracking revenue, costs, and expenses. But there's another crucial piece of the puzzle often left until the last minute or, worse, only fully addressed during the annual statutory audit: the Balance Sheet.

The Overlooked Balance Sheet

While the P&L tells you how well the company performed financially over the month, the Balance Sheet offers a snapshot of the company's financial position at a specific point in time. It reveals what the company owns and owes, which is just as critical for assessing the company's health and operational efficiency. Ignoring the Balance Sheet during monthly closings can hide significant financial insights and risks.

Why Monthly Balance Sheet Reviews Matter

1. ***Understanding Liabilities and Assets:*** Regularly reviewing the Balance Sheet helps track not only basic figures like cash at hand or debt levels but also more detailed items like ageing of debtors, creditors, and inventory levels. These items impact everything from cash flow to financial sustainability.

2. ***Detailed Breakup of Payable Accounts:*** Accounts such as expenses payable, salaries payable, taxes payable (like TDS), and other accrued expenses often build up without careful examination throughout the year. Regular reviews can prevent surprises and manage cash flow more effectively. For instance:
   - ***Expenses Payable/Provision of Expenses:*** Often a catch-all category, this account can become a "black box" of unsorted or forgotten items that can distort the understanding of actual liabilities.
   - ***Salaries Payable:*** Regular review ensures that any discrepancies in payroll are corrected promptly, maintaining accurate liability recording.
   - ***Taxes Payable:*** Ensuring taxes are correctly calculated and recorded monthly prevents year-end surprises and penalties.
3. ***Speeding Up the Statutory Audit:*** When Balance Sheet items are only reviewed in detail annually, it slows down the statutory audit process. If receivables, payables, and provisions are consistently reviewed and validated, the year-end audit becomes smoother and faster.
4. ***True Financial Health Assessment:*** Including the Balance Sheet in your monthly financial review provides a 360-degree view of your business's financial health. It shows not just how well you're earning, but also how effectively you're managing the resources and obligations you have.

Implementing Effective Monthly Balance Sheet Reviews

To ensure that your Balance Sheet receives the attention it deserves during monthly closures, consider these practical steps:

1. ***Schedule Regular Reviews:*** Just as you close your P&L, set a specific time each month dedicated to reviewing the Balance Sheet. Make it a part of your monthly financial routine.
2. ***Use Checklists:*** Create a checklist for Balance Sheet accounts review, similar to the procedures used for P&L. This helps ensure no item is overlooked and that everything is reviewed systematically.
3. ***Train Your Team:*** Make sure that your financial team understands the importance of the Balance Sheet and how to effectively review and analyze the information it contains. Regular training sessions can help reinforce this.
4. ***Leverage Technology:*** Utilize accounting software that can help streamline the reconciliation processes and provide real-time insights into various Balance Sheet items.
5. ***Foster Cross-Departmental Communication:*** Often, the information needed for accurate Balance Sheet entries might lie with other departments (like HR for salaries payable or the procurement department for creditors). Ensuring open lines of communication can lead to more accurate bookkeeping.

Conclusion

Expanding your monthly closing procedures to include a thorough review of the Balance Sheet not only enhances your understanding of your company's financial standing but also helps in proactive management of resources and obligations. It moves the finance department beyond compliance into the realm of strategic management, where each financial statement is a tool for deeper insight and smarter decision making.

● ● ● ●

Chapter 18

Streamlining the Audit Process through Regular Audit Schedule Updates

Have you ever felt the stress of preparing for the annual audit in finance and accounting? This time can be tough for everyone involved, especially as the audit date gets closer and preparations get intense, particularly around the audit schedule. But what if you could avoid this last-minute rush with some simple planning and regular updates? Let's look at why updating the audit schedule every month or quarter isn't just a good idea—it's a smart move.

Understanding the Static Nature of Business Operations

For many businesses, the day-to-day operations don't change drastically within a single financial year. Similarly, statutory auditors are often appointed for a period of five years, and their methods, barring regulatory updates, remain fairly consistent. Given these static aspects, continuously updating the audit schedule becomes not only feasible but also highly beneficial.

The Challenge of the Audit Schedule

The creation and preparation of the audit schedule in a specific format often represent one of the most time-consuming tasks during the statutory audit. Friction between the auditors and the company typically arises from delays in providing necessary information in the required formats. Auditors are under pressure to complete their work within a designated period, driven by the need to balance the relationship between time spent and the fees charged, and to meet regulatory or corporate deadlines.

The Strategic Benefits of Regular Updates

1. ***Early Detection of Inconsistencies:*** By updating the audit schedule monthly or quarterly, the Finance and Accounts team can continuously monitor and verify the data. This ongoing review helps in identifying and rectifying any inconsistencies or deficiencies long before the audit period, reducing last-minute surprises and stress.
2. ***Smoother Internal Audits:*** Regular updates to the audit schedule also facilitate smoother internal audits. With information being continually reviewed and adjusted, internal auditors find fewer issues, leading to quicker audits, fewer queries, and a higher level of trust and satisfaction with the financial reporting process.
3. ***Reduced Dependency on Key Personnel:*** In many companies, the departure of a key team member who handles audit preparations can cause significant disruptions. Regularly updated audit schedules mitigate this risk by ensuring that the company is not overly dependent on any single employee for audit readiness.
4. ***Efficiency During Statutory Audits:*** When the statutory audit rolls around, a well-maintained and regularly updated audit schedule means that much of the preliminary work is already done. This can significantly shorten the duration of the audit, reduce the workload on staff during the audit period, and decrease the overall stress and disruption to daily operations.

Applying the 80/20 Principle

We already discussed the 80/20 Principle in Chapter 7, but it's worth mentioning again here due to its importance.

While updating every part of the audit schedule may seem overwhelming, applying the Pareto Principle (or the 80/20 rule) can help make this task easier. Focus on the parts of the schedule that:

- Take up 80% of the time during audit preparations, or
- Are considered 80% critical by the auditors.

By prioritizing these key elements, the company can achieve most of the benefits of regular updates without overwhelming the team.

Conclusion

Updating the audit schedule on a regular basis is a proactive approach that can transform the annual audit from a fire drill into a well-orchestrated event. This practice not only ensures greater accuracy and readiness when the audit occurs but also builds a culture of continuous compliance and review within the finance team. It's about turning what used to be a reactive, stressful process into a strategic, controlled one, where surprises are minimized and the audit period can proceed with confidence and precision.

● ● ● ●

Chapter 19

Mastering the Accounts Payable Process Through Critical Tracking

For any business with a high volume of transactions, especially in sectors like manufacturing, managing the accounts payable (AP) process effectively is crucial. In a typical manufacturing company that handles around 4,000 invoices a month, keeping a finger on the pulse of accounts payable can mean the difference between financial fluidity and bottlenecks that can choke the entire operation.

Why Track Accounts Payable?

The AP department is more than just an administrative function; it's a hub of financial activity that affects cash flow, relationships with suppliers, and the overall financial health of a company. By tracking specific parameters of the accounts payable process, a company can gain valuable insights that lead to significant process improvements.

Key Parameters to Track in Accounts Payable

- *Volume of Transactions: PO vs. Non-PO*
  - Purchase Orders (POs) are pre-approved documents issued before receiving goods or services, while non-PO transactions may not require prior approval. Tracking the volume of PO versus Non-PO transactions helps in understanding the control environment and the predictability of cash outflows.

- ***Volume of Transactions: Urgent vs. Non-urgent***
  - Differentiating between urgent and non-urgent invoices is crucial. Urgent payments might disrupt the normal workflow and could indicate issues like poor planning, emergency purchases, or vendor demands. Analyzing this can help in streamlining purchase and payment procedures to avoid last-minute pressures.
- ***Volume of Transactions on Hold***
  - Invoices on hold represent a critical choke point in the AP process. Tracking these can highlight inefficiencies or systematic issues within the procurement or payment processes that need addressing to improve workflow and avoid late payment penalties.
- ***Major Reasons for Invoices Being on Hold***
  - Identifying why invoices are put on hold (e.g., discrepancies in amounts, missing information, awaiting approval) can pinpoint specific areas for process improvement, training, or perhaps even suggest a need for more automation.
- ***Turnaround Time or SLA for Invoice Processing***
  - Measuring the time from when an invoice is received to when it is processed (both booking and payment stages) provides insights into the efficiency of the AP department. This can be broken down further:
    - ***From Receipt to AP Team:*** How quickly are invoices passed from receipt at the company to the AP team?
    - ***AP Processing Time:*** Once with the AP team, how efficiently are invoices processed for booking and then payment?

Utilizing Data for Improvement and Automation

The data gathered from tracking these parameters isn't just for record-keeping. Here's how it can be actively used to drive change:

- ***Automation Opportunities:*** High volumes of routine, non-urgent PO invoices are prime candidates for automation. Automating these can reduce processing time, minimize errors, and free up staff for more complex tasks.
- ***Process Enhancements:*** Understanding the causes of delays and holds can lead to targeted process improvements, such as adjusting approval hierarchies or streamlining communications with vendors.
- ***Training Needs:*** If certain errors or delays are frequent, it might indicate a need for additional training or clearer guidelines for staff involved in the AP process.
- ***Vendor Relations:*** Regularly facing urgent invoices might necessitate renegotiating terms with suppliers or revising procurement strategies to better manage timelines and cash flow.

Conclusion

In essence, tracking critical parameters within the accounts payable process isn't just about keeping tabs on what's happening; it's about actively using this information to refine and enhance the system. For companies dealing with thousands of transactions monthly, these metrics provide a roadmap for where immediate improvements can be made and where strategic decisions must be focused to maintain a smooth, efficient, and cost-effective AP operation. This proactive approach not only optimizes accounts payable processes but also strengthens the overall financial foundation of the business.

Case study

A manufacturing company processing 3,000 invoices monthly faced significant delays, particularly with non-PO invoices that required additional verification.

Problem

Delays were frequent in the accounts payable (AP) process, with a substantial number of invoices regularly placed on hold, creating bottlenecks.

Solution Enhanced Tracking System

The company implemented a detailed tracking system to identify inefficiencies:

- ***PO vs. Non-PO Tracking:*** *The company tracked the timeliness of non-PO invoice submissions from various departments.*
- ***Hold Reasons:*** *They carefully recorded the reasons for invoices being placed on hold to address underlying issues.*

Implementation

- ***Data Collection and Analysis:*** *The company used software to automate tracking and categorize reasons for delays and holds.*
- ***Process Optimization:*** *New procedures were introduced to speed up the handling of non-PO invoices and resolve common issues causing holds.*

Results

- ***Reduced Processing Times:*** *The tracking insights led to significant reductions in invoice processing times.*
- ***Enhanced Transparency and Decision-Making:*** *The system provided clarity on AP processes, enabling quicker resolutions and less re-work.*
- ***Improved Employee and Vendor Relations:*** *Streamlined payments improved vendor relations, and clearer processes increased AP staff satisfaction and retention.*

Conclusion

Implementing a robust tracking system transformed the AP process by pinpointing and mitigating delays and inefficiencies. This not only enhanced operational efficiency but also bolstered financial stability and staff retention within the company.

● ● ● ●

Chapter 20

Harnessing the Power of Reminders in the Digital Age

How can the humble reminder, often overlooked in today's busy business landscape filled with distractions and short attention spans, become a silent hero in enhancing productivity and ensuring that nothing slips through the cracks? Whether integrated into email software like Outlook, Gmail, or Thunderbird, or set up on your smartphone, reminders are an essential tool waiting to be harnessed effectively.

The Decline of Our Memory Power

It's no secret that our ability to remember things has been affected by the digital environment surrounding us. With the constant buzz of notifications, the temptation of endless internet browsing, and the immediate demands of social media, our focus is more fragmented than ever. This environment makes it challenging to remember commitments, such as returning a phone call, or keeping track of critical tasks that aren't immediately pressing but are important nonetheless. For instance, how many times have we forgotten to call back a client or missed sending a crucial follow-up email because it simply slipped our minds?

The Critical Role of Reminders in Finance and Accounting

In the context of finance and accounting, the stakes of forgetting can be high. Compliance deadlines, quarterly reviews, payment due dates, and many other time-sensitive responsibilities make the finance department a high-pressure environment where the cost of forgetting is not just a missed call but potentially a compliance violation or a strained vendor relationship.

Recurring Tasks Automation

Many tasks in accounting are recurring, such as monthly account reconciliations, quarterly tax filings, and annual budget reviews. Setting up recurring reminders for these tasks can automate the process of remembering. Once set, these reminders ensure that no matter how busy the schedule or crowded the inbox, critical tasks do not get overlooked.

One-Time Reminders for Long-Term Tasks

Some tasks occur less frequently or require a follow-up in the distant future, such as renewing licenses, preparing for yearly audits, or following up on long-term financial strategies. Setting a one-time reminder for months or even a year in advance can ensure that these important tasks receive the attention they require exactly when needed, without the stress of keeping them top of mind at all times.

Expanding the Use of Reminders

Here are some practical ways to make the most of the reminder feature in both personal and professional settings:

- ***Integrate Reminders with Calendars:*** Most digital calendars offer the ability to set reminders for any event or task. Linking reminders with calendar entries can provide a visual cue and a time-specific nudge, enhancing the likelihood that the task will be completed.
- ***Use Task Management Tools:*** Many task and project management tools come with built-in reminder functions. These can be particularly useful for team-oriented tasks, providing reminders to all relevant team members.

- ***Smartphone Apps:*** Utilizing apps on smartphones for setting reminders can also be highly effective, especially for on-the-go professionals. These apps can send notifications directly to your phone, ensuring you're alerted regardless of whether you're in front of a computer.
- ***Email Follow-Ups:*** For tasks that involve communication, setting reminders to follow up on emails can keep conversations from going dormant, especially when waiting on a response is crucial.

Conclusion

In an age where digital distractions are the norm, reminders serve as an anchor, keeping our responsibilities within reach and our tasks on track. For finance professionals, where precision and timeliness are paramount, leveraging reminders can transform the workflow, reduce stress, and ensure a smooth operational cadence. So, make the most of digital reminders to stay focused, be punctual, and never miss a beat in the fast-paced world of finance and accounting.

● ● ● ●

Chapter 21

Mastering Team Planning for Finance and Accounting

In finance, effective team planning is not just a good practice—it's essential. While individual planning allows each team member to manage their workload according to their personal style, team-level planning ensures that everyone's efforts are synchronized and that the entire team is moving toward common goals efficiently and effectively.

The Importance of Team Planning

Good planning simplifies execution. This is a truth understood in all areas of business, but it holds particular weight in finance and accounting where deadlines are tight and regulations are strict. Without a cohesive team plan, individual efforts, while well-intentioned, may not align, leading to friction and inefficiencies.

Monthly and Quarterly Planning Sessions

It's advisable for finance and accounting teams to hold formal planning sessions on a monthly and quarterly basis. These sessions serve multiple purposes:

- ***Visibility and Transparency:*** When team members share their schedules and work plans, it helps everyone understand the workload and responsibilities of their colleagues. This visibility can prevent bottlenecks and overloads by allowing for adjustments before issues arise.

- ***Anticipating and Managing Surprises:*** Regular planning meetings help identify potential conflicts early on. Knowing when a team member has a heavy load allows the team to redistribute work proactively or provide additional support, thus maintaining workflow continuity.
- ***Enhancing Team Communication:*** These sessions promote open dialogue among team members, enhancing understanding and cooperation. They also provide a forum for discussing potential challenges and brainstorming solutions collectively.
- ***Monitoring Commitment and Competence:*** For CFOs and team leaders, these planning sessions are an opportunity to observe and assess the commitment and competence of team members. Understanding who meets deadlines, who needs more resources, and who consistently takes on more responsibilities can inform decisions about promotions, team restructuring, and professional development.

Integrating Leave Planning

One critical component that should always be included in these planning sessions is leave planning. Understanding when team members plan to take leave is crucial for several reasons:

- ***Work Continuity:*** Knowing about planned absences in advance allows the team to arrange for coverage or adjust project timelines accordingly. This planning ensures that all functions continue smoothly, even in someone's absence.
- ***Stakeholder Communication:*** Early awareness of team members' leaves allows for better communication with other departments and external stakeholders. If someone responsible for a critical report or presentation will be unavailable, stakeholders can be informed in advance, and alternative arrangements can be made.
- ***Reducing Workload Stress:*** Effective leave planning prevents scenarios where team members return to a piled-up workload,

which can be stressful and counterproductive. It ensures that work is evenly distributed and managed during their absence.

Implementation of Effective Team Planning

To make these planning sessions as effective as possible, consider the following strategies:

- ***Regular Scheduling:*** Hold these meetings at consistent intervals (e.g., the last Friday of every month) so that they become a routine part of the team's workflow.
- ***Structured Agendas:*** Develop a standard agenda for these meetings that includes updates from each team member, a review of upcoming deadlines, a discussion of any potential issues, and leave planning.
- ***Inclusive Atmosphere:*** Encourage all team members to participate actively. This not only enhances the quality of the planning but also fosters a sense of ownership and accountability among the team.
- ***Documentation and Follow-Up:*** Ensure that the outcomes of these meetings are documented and accessible to all team members. Assign action items where necessary, and follow up on these items in the next meeting.

Conclusion

Incorporating comprehensive planning sessions into the routine of finance and accounting teams can significantly transform how these teams operate. By fostering transparency, anticipating challenges, and coordinating effectively, these sessions enable smoother operations, better workload management, and a more cohesive team dynamic. Thus, mastering team planning is not just about organizing work; it's about enhancing the team's overall effectiveness and job satisfaction.

● ● ● ●

Conclusion - Ensuring Excellence in Accounting and Compliance

As we close this comprehensive guide on "Bulletproof Accounting and Compliance," it's clear that the role of the Chief Financial Officer and their teams has never been more crucial. The twenty-one proven strategies we've explored provide a blueprint for CFOs committed to enhancing their departments, ensuring accuracy, fostering efficiency, and upholding stringent compliance standards. This conclusion aims to encapsulate the core principles that should guide every finance professional's action and to inspire continued excellence and innovation in the field.

Embracing a Proactive Approach

Throughout this book, a recurring theme has been the importance of a proactive rather than reactive approach. Whether it's implementing robust planning practices, staying ahead of compliance requirements, or fostering continuous professional development, the goal is clear: anticipate challenges before they become problems. By staying proactive, CFOs can not only safeguard their organizations against potential pitfalls but also seize opportunities for growth and improvement.

Fostering Team Collaboration and Communication

Another pillar of effective financial management is fostering a culture of open communication and collaboration within the finance team and across the organization. As we've seen, the integration of regular planning sessions, the strategic use of technology for enhancing communication, and the encouragement of a team-oriented approach to problem-solving can significantly boost productivity and morale. When team members understand their roles and the impact of their work on the organization's broader goals, they are more engaged and committed to delivering their best.

Leveraging Technology Wisely

Using technology wisely is crucial in modern finance functions. From automating routine tasks to employing sophisticated analytics for strategic decision-making, technology can drastically enhance the efficiency and accuracy of financial operations. However, as we've discussed, it's crucial to approach technology as a tool to augment—not replace—the human elements of insight, judgement, and ethical considerations.

Commitment to Continuous Improvement

Continuous improvement is the bedrock upon which long-term success is built. This involves not only refining existing processes and systems but also committing to ongoing education and development of the finance team. By encouraging a mindset of lifelong learning and staying abreast of the latest industry trends and regulatory changes, CFOs can ensure their teams remain competent and competitive.

Ethical Leadership and Integrity

Above all, the role of a CFO demands a steadfast commitment to ethical leadership and integrity. The finance function relies heavily on trust from stakeholders, and it is the responsibility of every finance professional to uphold the highest standards of honesty and ethical behavior. This trust is the foundation of a company's reputation and is critical to its long-term success.

Conclusion

The journey to bulletproof your accounting and compliance functions is ongoing and dynamic. Each of the twenty-one strategies discussed in this book serves as a stepping stone towards building a more robust, efficient, and transparent finance department. By adopting these practices, CFOs and their teams can not only meet the challenges of today's complex business environment but also lay the groundwork for future success.

In this ever-evolving landscape, remember that each small step taken to improve processes, each effort made to foster team collaboration, and every decision guided by integrity contributes to the greater goal of excellence. Let this book serve not just as a manual for best practices but as a source of inspiration to innovate, lead, and succeed in the noble pursuit of guiding your organization to financial and ethical excellence.

● ● ● ●

Your Next Step in Financial Excellence

As a CFO, you are at the heart of driving strategy, ensuring compliance, and safeguarding the financial health of your organization. Yet, challenges in the Finance & Accounts function—be it inefficiencies, resource constraints, or compliance complexities—can derail even the best-laid plans. Over the last two decades, having worked with more than 200 companies across industries, we have gained invaluable insights into overcoming these obstacles effectively.

This book has shared actionable strategies to bulletproof your accounting and compliance processes. Now, we invite you to take the next step: Partner with us to ensure your finance operations not only thrive but are future-ready.

If you're facing challenges in your Finance & Accounts function, here's how we can help:

- **Consulting Services:** We can act as your trusted advisor to diagnose challenges and recommend practical, tailored solutions. Whether it's optimizing processes, setting up KPIs, or improving compliance, we deliver strategies that align with your unique needs.
- **Outsourced Accounting and Compliance Services:** We can manage your accounting and compliance processes through an offsite model, taking care of bookkeeping, financial reporting, and statutory compliance so you can focus on strategic priorities.

Why Work with Us?

- **Proven Expertise:** Decades of experience across industries, solving real-world challenges.
- **Practical Solutions:** Implementable strategies that deliver measurable results.
- **Cost-Effective Models:** Save time and resources while maintaining high standards.
- **Customization:** Flexible services designed to meet your specific requirements.

By partnering with us, you'll gain not only solutions but also the time and bandwidth to focus on strategic growth, team development, and achieving your business goals.

Know More About Us

Curious to learn more?

About Chandan Goyal

Discover the journey, expertise, and insights of Chandan Goyal.

Scan the QR code below to know more.

About Blue Consulting

Explore how Blue Consulting has been empowering businesses with cutting-edge accounting, compliance, and finance solutions for over two decades.

Scan the QR code below to learn more.

● ● ● ●

www.ingramcontent.com/pod-product-compliance
Ingram Content Group UK Ltd.
Pitfield, Milton Keynes, MK11 3LW, UK
UKHW022006190726
13853UKWH00004B/1771

9 789363 385931